The Beginners Guide to a Profitable Hemp Farm

Table of Contents

Introduction 1

1. Begin With the Tough Questions 3

2. What's the Win? Creating a Business Plan. 10

3. Have a Plan B, C, and D 14

4. Find Experts for Advice 17

5. Make Friends With Local Farmers 20

6. Working With Processors and Buyers 22

Conclusion 28

Glossary of Terms 30

About the Author 34

Introduction

Hemp is hot right now. Many new farmers are seeing the massive opportunity, and getting involved.

The problem is many don't know the first thing about the market and end up losing their shorts.

It doesn't have to be this way.

Farming hemp can be lucrative. The potential is there. But that is all it is: Potential. Until you have received payment for your crop, your beautiful 12% CBD biomass is nothing more than potential.

Since nothing is guaranteed in hemp farming, you as a hemp farmer are incurring risk.

I am a hemp farmer, work for a processor, have co-created an online hemp farming course, and have created my own CBD products. This eBook comes as a result of working with many farmers and seeing the costly mistakes many have made. My goal is to help you avoid the pitfalls that could devastate your farm and finances, and turn your risk into a profitable hemp farming business.

For some, this book will steer you away from hemp farming. That may be the best thing for you. If your small investment in this book helps you to see that hemp farming is not for you, it could potentially save you tens of thousands of dollars.

If you decide to take the plunge after reading this book, you will be informed on how to mitigate risk and will be more prepared to have a successful and profitable season.

To a profitable hemp farming season!

Chapter 1

———— ও৯০৯৯ ————

Begin With the Tough Questions

When you first decide to explore the opportunity of farming hemp, you need to be able to assess your resources to see if you can pull it off. Many farmers decide to jump into hemp farming without taking the time to consider the cost. This is an expensive way to learn.

My goal in this chapter is to throw a bunch of questions at you. I want you to take a notepad, and write down your answers to these questions because they will be the framework for your business plan.

1. What land will you be using for farming?

Land is important. If you own the land, you are at an advantage. Before you do anything, you should test your soil to see the Ph and what kind of nutrients are currently in the soil. This will allow you to amend the soil before you plant. The soil should be a sandy loom with excellent drainage.

2. Do you have the financial resources to pull it off?

There are a lot of costs involved in farming hemp, especially if you are a first time farmer. I recommend budgeting $10,000 per acre. This includes seeds, plastic mulch, drip tape, fertilizer, miscellaneous materials, and labor.

There are several other things that you will need, that could increase your budget per acre if you do not already have access to them. I have created a PDF that you can download that will give you a monthly farming timeline and per-acre budget planner. You can download it for free at HempFarmingAcademy.com/timeline.

If you are farming anything over 1 acre, you will want a tractor with at least 40HP to lay the plastic mulch pull the water wheel transplanter when transplanting your seedlings. You could choose to farm without plastic, and plant by hand, but you will need a lot of manpower to stay on top of the weeds and plant by hand.

3. Where will you source your hemp seeds?

I don't want to use this book to endorse any seed company specifically, but I will tell you what to look for because not all hemp seeds are created equal. You want seeds that have a high germination rate (above 90%) and a high feminization rate (higher than 99%).

During the flowering stage, you will pull your male plants so that they do not pollinate your female plants. If your female plants get pollinated, they will give their energy to producing seeds instead of CBD. This will devalue your crop since you are going for the highest CBD potency possible.

It is a good idea to find a reputable company with a few years' track record of producing high CBD plants. Request a CoA (Certificate of Analysis) to see lab tests performed on the seeds. These lab tests will help you understand if they are producing high CBD plants.

Another good idea is to ask other farmers what genetics they are using. Find out what has worked for them in the past. If you ask the right questions, you will be more prepared to make an informed decision on the best genetics for your farm.

4. Is there sufficient water rights for the amount of hemp you want to grow?

The hemp plant doesn't require much water, but in the peak part of the season, you will need to budget about 1 gallon per plant per day. This can be several hours of watering per day through a drip system.

5. Is your farm located in a region that is good for farming hemp?

Since hemp is a crop that is dependent on the light cycle, being near the 45th parallel is ideal. This will provide around 18 hours of sunlight at the summer solstice. Once the days start getting shorter, your hemp plant will transition from the vegetative stage to the flowering stage. It is at this time the plant will focus on producing CBD rich flowers.

6. How will you dry your plants?

Of course, the plants need to be dried before the CBD oil can be extracted. Most processors want the plant to be less than 10% moisture. You can choose to accomplish this naturally or mechanically.

If you live in a region that is very dry and doesn't get a lot of rainfall in the Autumn months, field drying is an option. If not, you will need to make sure that you have adequate space to hang dry your plants. You will roughly need 35,000 cubic feet per acre to hang dry. Make sure your structure can bear the weight of this many plants.

Another option is to machine dry your plants. Many groups are offering this service. This can be very costly, and as a fan of keeping costs low, I do not recommend this method unless you already have access to the equipment. It could eat into your profits.

If you don't have a solid drying plan at the beginning of the season, you could be forced into machine drying to save your crop, so be sure to work thisced fore you plant.

7. Are you planning on doing all the work yourself, or will you hire labor?

The answer to this question depends on how many acres you are farming and how hard you want to work. The two most time-consuming parts of the farming process are planting and harvesting, so you may want to get a team together for these stages. If you are hang drying your plants, this is very time-consuming. As a ballpark estimate, it will take about 40 man-hours per acre to hang dry your plants.

If you are planning on selling biomass, you will need to shuck the plant. Whether you choose to do this by hand, or with a combine or other stripping method, you will probably need to get help for this stage too. If you are wanting to combine your plants to biomass, and don't own a combine, prepare to budget about $1500 per acre to hire this out.

If you are planning on selling flower, hand trimming is very time-consuming. Plan on paying a team by the hour to help with hand trimming. There is a lot of labor involved in the harvest, so expect to work hard or put it into your budget.

Chapter 2

What's the Win? Creating a Business Plan.

Now that you have answered the tough questions, it is time to create a business plan. Your business plan will highlight your goals, strategies, and your financial plan to reach the finish line successfully.

Your business plan doesn't need to be a huge publication, but it is a good idea to get your plan on paper so you can execute it properly. Of course, things don't always go according to plan, so it is good to think through a plan B, C, and D.

Here are some of the fundamental elements you want to include in your business plan.

1. Business Overview
This section will include your Executive Summary which will be a few short paragraphs explaining

the who, what, when, where and why of your farm. You can also include your mission, core values, and objectives in this section. This will help you think through what is important to you, and the specific goals you have for the season.

2. Market Analysis

You want to get this section right because a realistic view of the current market will help you plan properly and have accurate expectations for the profitability of your farm. If your understanding of the current market for hemp is off, you will have a rude awakening come harvest time. Research the going rate for biomass and trimmed flower. Outline your target market, and your sales strategy to get paid for your product.

3. S.W.O.T. Analysis

In your SWOT analysis, you will think through the strengths, weaknesses, opportunities, and threats for your hemp farming business. Be very objective in this step, and ask for feedback from any trusted advisors. This step will help you think through hurdles that could arise so that you have a solution before you need it.

4. Management Summary

In this section, you will address who is doing what in your business, and who owns what percentage of the business. If there is split ownership in the business, it is a good idea to have a lawyer work out a partnership agreement so that everyone is on the same page before you get started.

5. Financial Plan

Farming hemp is unique to other businesses in that there is a lot of investment upfront and no payoff until it is all over. How are you financing your farm? Create an exhaustive list of expenses that you will have throughout the year so that you can understand your total budget and acquire the proper financing if needed. In this section, you should also address the expected revenue generated from your crop. The more you can plan on the front end, the more prepared you will be throughout the season.

Your business plan can be used as a tool to acquire financing for the farm. If nothing else, it will be a good exercise for you to think through the entire year, what you will need, potential hurdles to overcome, and how much money you expect to earn from your efforts.

Farming is a risk, and there will be curveballs thrown at you every day. Anticipating these obstacles, and solving problems is a big part of what farming is all about.

If you don't remember anything else from this book, remember this: KEEP YOUR EXPENSES LOW! Do a good job, and don't cut corners...but give yourself as much margin as possible. In other words, don't buy new tractors and hire out expensive services in your first year as many other farmers have. This adds a lot of unnecessary stress when it comes time to sell your crop.

Chapter 3

Have a Plan B, C, and D

In the last chapter, we talked about creating a business plan before you get started. While this is an extremely important exercise, it is also important to recognize that things rarely go according to plan. And that is why it is important to have contingencies lined up when things go sideways.

Farming Contingencies

Every step of farming may not go according to plan, so it is important to be ready.

When your plan A seed company sells out of their seeds before you were able to purchase, what other seed companies do you feel comfortable with?

When your irrigation components are on backorder for 2 months because of the high demand, what are you going to do?
When your tractor breaks down on planting day, how will you transplant into the field?

When mites, or deer, or hail attack your plants, what will you do?

When you run out of storage, how will you dry the rest of your plants?

I couldn't possibly name all of the potential issues you may encounter farming. As a farmer, you need to be a good problem solver with a lot of patience. Anticipate the issues and figure out solutions before they arise, and you will be in good shape.

Financial Contingencies

Most farmers that grow hemp do it because of the potential financial reward. It is true, hemp farming has been lucrative for many farmers across the country. But nothing is guaranteed. What happens when the going rate for biomass takes a nosedive? What if your contracted buyer drops out and can't purchase your product?

Plan B could be to enter into a product or revenue split with an extractor if the market is not allowing them to purchase your biomass/flower for cash.

Plan B might include creating your own CBD products to sell. Consumer products are much more profitable than hemp, but it could mean more time and investment to get there.

This is why it is really important to keep your expenses low. Keeping your expenses low allows you margin to accept a lower price for your product (if needed) without going under.

I hope these scenarios don't happen to you. But if you plan for the worst, and you have a great season, this just means more money in your bank account.

Chapter 4

———— ❧❦❧ ————

Find Experts for Advice

Farming Hemp is not rocket science. But if it is your first time, it is important to have knowledgeable people on speed dial.

If you are not an expert with water flow and irrigation, find a supplier that will take the time to come to your farm and help you strategize your irrigation system. They will be able to calculate your water pressure and set you up with a good system that will work for years to come.

Another valuable person to have around is an agronomist. This is someone who has gone to college to study the science of soil management and crop production and will know the ins and outs of how to feed your plants. Often your local agricultural fertilizer company will have an agronomist on staff. They should be able to set you up with a fertilization plan for hemp that will be high on the Nitrogen during the vegetative stage, with a transition to Phosphorous and Potassium during the flowering stage. If you are using a drip irrigation system, you can feed your plants with a liquid mixture as you water your plants straight through the drip tape.

As a first time farmer, you are on a quest for the information that will work for your farm. Visit hemp conferences, educational opportunities, and speak with other farmers that have a couple of years under their belt. It is my firm belief that if you ask the right questions to enough people, you will get the answers you need to be successful.

That said, take everything you hear with a grain of salt, and get multiple opinions. You will find that everyone has a different opinion of how to farm this crop, and there are a lot of nut-jobs out there that don't know what they are talking about. If you get the same advice multiple times, and it makes sense to you, chances are it is.

Learn to trust your gut when it comes to your farming relationships. There are a lot of folks in this industry that cannot be trusted, so keep your eyes open for BS.

Chapter 5

————  ————

Make Friends With Local Farmers

Some people look at other farmers as their competition. I think this is stupid, arrogant, and won't get you anywhere. The reality is, we need each other.

Some of the greatest people I have worked with (and became close friends with) are my neighboring farmers. You can learn from them, network with them, and potentially share equipment with them.

All of us are trying to reach the same goal, and sometimes you will be more successful by being part of a pack instead of a lone wolf.

The key here is to be a person of integrity. Legitimately care for your neighboring farms, and make yourself available to help. When they see that you are not in it just for yourself, they will reciprocate.

Neighboring farmers may have good information about what strains of seeds work best in your location. They may have a network of buyers that you could tap into. They will also know who to contact for help when it comes to fertilizer, and soil tests, and irrigation, etc.

I have learned a lot from just talking to other farmers, and they have learned some things from me. I am kind, helpful, and as a result, they feel they can trust me. Trust goes a long way and has proven to be helpful on several occasions.

Chapter 6

———— ❧❦❦❧ ————

Working With Processors and Buyers

The mistake that many farmers make is they wait until harvest to find a buyer for their crop. By this time, most processers are already at capacity with contracts.

If you are growing for biomass to process into concentrated CBD oil, you need to begin developing relationships with processors in your region early. Some will even be willing to sign a futures contract with you before you plant, or early in the season. This contract would include an agreed-upon price that is contingent on the potency of your crop. In other words, they will pay if you deliver.

Even if you aren't able to obtain a futures contract, make sure the CEO of the Extraction facility knows you by name. Check-in with them periodically. Don't be annoying, because they are very busy, and have a business to run as well. But if you are the first face that pops up in their mind come harvest time, this will put you in a great position. Do this with several extraction facilities so that if your plan A falls through, you have other places to take your biomass.

Getting Paid

As a hemp farmer, you have a couple of possible products you could sell: biomass and/or flower. Typically you sell biomass to a processor that will extract and sell the oil wholesale in kilogram or liter quantities.

Hemp flower, on the other hand, is usually sold to a wholesale buyer that will resell it in smaller retail quantities for a profit.

Biomass

In my opinion, the way the industry pays for biomass is kind of broken, but let me explain how it works.

Generally speaking, a processor will pay a farmer for their biomass with this equation: Dry Weight (pounds) x CBD % x Going Rate = Price. For example, 1000 pounds of 9% CBD biomass at a rate of $2.50 would be $22,500 (1000 x 9 x 2.25 = 22,500) or $22.50 per pound.

Although this is the main way the industry places a monetary value on biomass, it is not the most reliable system. A lot of money is riding on a biomass core sample test measuring the CBD potency of the biomass (usually rounded up or down). If you are selling tens of thousands of pounds of biomass, a partial percentage point could be the difference of thousands of dollars.

In addition, the sample(s) that are taken for testing the biomass may not be representative of the whole batch. That said, it is the way most of the industry pays for biomass right now, so I wanted to include this so that you know what to expect.

I believe biomass value will one day be calculated by actual oil yields from the extraction process. This method, although more reliable in theory, places a lot of trust that the extraction facility is being truthful about the extraction numbers.

Hemp Flower

Price for Hemp Flower is a little more straight forward: A simple agreed-upon price per pound. CBD potency doesn't have a lot to do with the value. The quality of the flower is determined more by the look and smell. Trimmed hemp flower has been averaging around $300 (Give or take $100) per pound in recent years.

Splits Explained

Something that you need to understand is that most processors don't have millions of dollars sitting around for the acquisition of biomass. As a result, many processors offer a split deal. Typically, there are two types of splits; a *revenue* split, and a *product* split.

In a revenue split, the processor extracts your biomass into oil or isolate, sells the oil/isolate, and splits the revenue with you. If the processor has purchase orders for their wholesale CBD oil extract, a revenue split can be lucrative for both parties. If they do not have buyers for the oil, it may take longer than expected to get paid and can be very frustrating.

In a product split, the processor agrees to extract your biomass in exchange for a percentage of your crop. In other words, you give them all your crop for processing, and you get a percentage of the CBD oil or isolate back. You can sell the oil yourself or make products out of it. Since the CBD oil concentrate is more valuable than your biomass, this could be a good deal for you if you have a buyer. Be sure to research what licenses and tests are required in your state to handle CBD concentrate, and sell it.

Before entering into a split agreement, make sure you understand WHEN your biomass will be processed, and WHEN you can expect payment. Getting paid a month after harvest is much better than 8 months after harvest.

Like I have said in previous chapters, make sure you trust your gut when working with processors, and make sure you understand the contract you sign. The contract should have a payment date, with interest owed if the processor does not fulfill their end of the deal.

If you are selling your trimmed flower, the same rules apply. Make sure that everything is above board and in writing.

Conclusion

I trust this short eBook has been a helpful reference to help you get started on the right foot with hemp farming. If you have decided to farm hemp this year, and still need some hand-holding along the way, I have another resource that can take you to the next level and ensure a profitable hemp farming season. It is an online course that I co-created with world-renowned cannabis farmer, Tom Lauerman. In this online course, we teach everything from field preparation, to seed germination, planting, all the way through harvest. To enroll in the course, all you have to do is visit HempFarmingAcademy.com and click one of the buttons to sign up.

I want to conclude by encouraging you on your journey. Hemp Farming is so much fun! It is a beautiful plant that does so much good for our planet and our health.

I have made lifelong friends, and have been able to share in the joy of other farmer's success.

Finally, it has been a tool to teach my teenage boys about long days and hard work. They have got their hands dirty in the field, learned about heavy machinery, and have helped me bottle and label our own CBD products. They are part of the entire process, and can take pride in the profits…that will pay for their college!

I wish you success with large colas and high CBD potency!

Glossary of Terms

Cannabinoids – The chemical compounds found in the cannabis plant that gives the plant its value and are used as natural medicine. There are over 100 known cannabinoids contained in the hemp plant. CBD and THC are the most well-known and studied cannabinoids.

CBD – Stands for 'cannabidiol' which is one of the many cannabinoids in hemp, and has been shown to treat pain, anxiety, & as a sleep aid to name a few. CBD genetics are bred to yield high percentages of CBD in their plants.

THC – Short for 'tetrahydrocannabinol', this cannabinoid is the main psychoactive chemical that causes the "high" sensation in marijuana. The current legal limit for THC in hemp and hemp-derived products is .3%.

Biomass – Hemp Biomass refers to bulk dried plant material (minus stalks and stems) intended for processing to produce hemp oil, & CBD extracts. Biomass is typically chipped or milled, and stored in large sacks.

Flower – The flower is the part of the plant that contains the bulk of the cannabinoids, oil, and terpenes.

Crude oil – The initial oil that is extracted from the whole plant.

Distillate – Distillate is CBD oil that has been heavily refined and separated into a higher concentrated cannabinoid oil.

Isolate – A white crystalline byproduct of distillate produced through a process to isolate CBD.

THC-Free Distillate – A distilled oil that has the THC removed to a non-detect level.

Winterization – The process to remove lipids and waxes from the crude oil. This step removes impurities in the raw crude oil and is more desirable to some in the crude oil market. It is also an important step before distillation because it will help create a more purified and transparent distillate.

Full-spectrum – A term used to describe oil that is the byproduct of the whole plant, without removing any cannabinoids.

Broad-spectrum – A term used to describe oil that has been more refined, usually to remove THC.

Toll Processing – When the farmer pays the processor to process the hemp biomass to oil or isolate.

Revenue Splits – The processor extracts oil from the biomass, sells the oil/isolate, and the farmer and processor split the revenue from the oil/isolate sale.

Product Splits – The processor retains agreed upon biomass as payment to process the biomass for the farmer. The farmer will receive his portion of the processed oil.

Processor – The words processor and extractor are used interchangeably. They refer to the facility that extracts CBD oil from hemp biomass.

Made in the USA
Middletown, DE
14 September 2024

60960607R00021